Money Makers
Building Wealth with Small Business and Investment Strategies

Table of Contents

1. Introduction 1

2. Understanding the Basics of Financial Stability 2

    2.1. Fundamentals of Financial Stability 2

    2.2. The Importance of Budgeting 3

    2.3. Understanding Debt 3

    2.4. Establishing an Emergency Fund 4

    2.5. Planning for Retirement 4

    2.6. Investing For Financial Growth 4

    2.7. Insuring Your Financial Future 5

3. Foundations of Small Business Management 6

    3.1. Management: A Core Component 6

    3.2. Small Business: The Unique Challenges 7

    3.3. Entrepreneurship: The Spirit of Small Business 8

        3.3.1. Traits of Successful Entrepreneurs 8

    3.4. Legal Structures of Small Businesses 8

    3.5. Financing and Capital Management 9

    3.6. Early Stage and Rapid Growth 9

4. Business Planning and Strategy Development 11

    4.1. The Significance of Business Planning 11

    4.2. Components of a Successful Business Plan 11

    4.3. The Process of Building a Business Plan 12

    4.4. Strategy Development: More than Just Planning 13

    4.5. The Process of Developing a Business Strategy 14

5. Mastering Cash Flow in Small Businesses 15

    5.1. Understanding Cash Flow 15

    5.2. Cash Flow Analysis 15

    5.3. Improving Cash Flows 16

    5.4. Cash Flow Forecasting 17

5.5. Building a Cash Reserve 18

6. Modern Investment Models and Their Implications 19

   6.1. The Efficient Market Hypothesis 19

   6.2. The Capital Asset Pricing Model 20

   6.3. Modern Portfolio Theory 20

   6.4. The Black-Scholes Model 20

   6.5. Artificial Intelligence and Machine Learning 21

   6.6. Implications of Modern Investment Models 21

7. Unlocking the Power of the Stock Market 23

   7.1. The Basics of Stock Market Investing 23

   7.2. Fundamental Analysis Vs. Technical Analysis 24

   7.3. The Art of Diversification 24

   7.4. Implementing Stop-Loss Orders 25

   7.5. Rebalancing Your Portfolio 25

8. Real Estate Investment: A Goldmine in Disguise 26

   8.1. The Concept of Real Estate Investment 26

   8.2. Why Real Estate Investment 26

   8.3. Different Methods of Real Estate Investing 27

   8.4. Assessing a Real Estate Investment 28

9. Estate Planning and Wealth Preservation 29

   9.1. Understanding Estate Planning 29

   9.2. The Importance of Last Will and Testament 29

   9.3. Utilizing Trusts in Estate Planning 30

   9.4. Planning for Incapacity 30

   9.5. Tax Implications and Estate Planning 30

   9.6. Assets Not Subject to Estate Plan 31

   9.7. Implementing Buy-Sell Agreements for Business Owners . . . 31

   9.8. Regular Reviews and Updates of Your Estate Plan 31

10. Crypto-assets: Navigating the New Frontiers of Investment 33

   10.1. Understanding Cryptocurrencies 33

10.2. Blockchain: The Underpinning Technology 34

10.3. Investing in Cryptocurrencies 34

10.4. Diversifying Portfolio with Crypto-assets 35

10.5. Bitcoin & Beyond: Evaluating Crypto-assets 35

10.6. Navigating Crypto Exchanges 36

11. Building a Diverse and Resilient Investment Portfolio 37

11.1. The Concept of Diversification 37

11.2. How Diversification Works 37

11.3. Importance of a Diverse Portfolio 38

11.4. Building a Diverse Portfolio 38

11.5. The Concept of Resilience in Investments 39

11.6. Building a Resilient Portfolio 39

Chapter 1. Introduction

Unlock your financial potential with our Special Report: "Money Makers: Building Wealth with Small Business and Investment Strategies". This comprehensive guide provides an exciting opportunity for you to spearhead your wealth-building journey starting from small business management to mastering advanced investment strategies. It's packed with practical steps, easy-to-understand guidelines, and real-life success stories that will undeniably inspire you to make the first step. Whether you're an absolute beginner or someone looking to diversify their income stream, this report is your gateway to a more secure and prosperous financial future. Embark on this compelling journey towards achieving financial independence and let your money work for you! It's time to think big, start small and scale fast, ready?

Chapter 2. Understanding the Basics of Financial Stability

The journey towards financial stability starts by understanding its basic tenets. In its simplest form, financial stability refers to the state wherein all finances are relatively stable and sustained, where income meets expenses, debts are well-managed, and a healthy amount of savings is maintained.

2.1. Fundamentals of Financial Stability

Financial stability doesn't just happen. It is the product of careful planning, smart choices, and self-discipline. It revolves around a few core principles:

1. Earning: The starting point of financial stability is having a consistent source of income to cover daily living expenses. This might be through employment, your small business, or investments.

2. Saving: After earning, it's essential to save a part of your income for future use. A rule of thumb – aim to save at least 20% of your income.

3. Spending: Responsible spending ensures that your income isn't wasted on unnecessary expenses. Prioritize needs over wants and cultivate frugal habits.

4. Investing: This is the ultimate way to grow your wealth. Invest in opportunities that yield a return over time, such as real estate, stock market, or mutual funds.

5. Managing Debt: Minimize and manage debts to maintain financial health. Keep credit usage minimal and pay off your

balances in full whenever possible.

2.2. The Importance of Budgeting

Creating and sticking to a budget is one of the most fundamental elements of financial stability. It guides your spending and helps you track where your money is going. Start by calculating your net income - the money you actually take home after taxes and other deductions. Then, list your monthly expenses, both fixed and variable. Compare income against expenses to see whether you're living within your means.

If your expenses exceed income, it's time to make some adjustments. Cut down on non-essential expenses and aim to increase your savings progressively. Remember, the goal of budgeting is to make sure you can comfortably cover all costs, save for the future, and still enjoy life today.

2.3. Understanding Debt

Debt can be a useful tool when used responsibly but can also be a slippery slope into financial instability if not managed properly. There are two types of debt: good debt and bad debt. "Good" debt refers to money borrowed to invest in something that will increase in value or generate long-term income. A mortgage, for example, is often considered good debt. "Bad" debt is anything that doesn't enhance your financial position or has depreciating value, such as a luxurious vacation financed on credit.

To maintain financial stability, it's crucial to keep bad debt to a minimum and manage good debt effectively. Always ensure your debt-to-income ratio (debt payments divided by gross income) stays below 36%.

2.4. Establishing an Emergency Fund

Unexpected expenses can push anyone towards financial instability. This is why an emergency fund is vital. It's recommended to have about three to six months' worth of living expenses set aside in a readily available account.

This fund serves as a financial safety net, so in case of sudden job loss, medical emergencies, car repairs, or other unforeseen expenses, you don't have to borrow money or dip into your long-term investments.

2.5. Planning for Retirement

Your working years serve as the foundation for financial stability in retirement. Begin by considering how much you'll need to maintain your lifestyle in retirement. Consider various income sources such as social security, pension, retirement savings accounts, and investment returns.

It's crucial to start contributing toward your retirement as early as possible, leveraging compound interest. The earlier you start, the more time your money has to grow.

2.6. Investing For Financial Growth

Investing is essentially turning your money into more money. It's a crucial element in achieving financial stability as it allows your wealth to grow over time. Start by understanding the different types of investments - stocks, bonds, mutual funds, real estate, etc., and how each can contribute to your wealth-building strategy. Always remember the golden rule of investing: never invest money that you can't afford to lose.

2.7. Insuring Your Financial Future

Insurance is about protection - it safeguards you from financial setbacks that come with life's unexpected events. Whether it's health insurance, life insurance, homeowner's insurance, or car insurance, having the right coverage is an essential part of financial stability. It takes care of potential losses and helps you stay financially stable even when unforeseen circumstances occur.

Financial stability might seem like a daunting journey, but understanding its basics and implementing them in your financial practices can lead to a more secure future. Remember, the journey to financial stability involves making informed decisions, taking calculated risks, and maintaining discipline in spending, saving, and investing practices.

Chapter 3. Foundations of Small Business Management

To successfully navigate the realm of small business management, one needs to understand its foundational principles. Having a strong foundation will provide you with a robust framework on which to base your decisions further down the line.

3.1. Management: A Core Component

Management, at its most basic level, refers to the process of planning, organizing, leading, and controlling resources—be it human, financial, physical, or informational—to achieve organizational goals. In essence, it's about doing and getting things done through people. As a small business owner, you are the principal manager and thus, responsible for all these aspects.

Effective management can be broken down into five primary functions: planning, organizing, staffing, leading, and controlling. In small businesses, these functions often overlap, and the business owner will typically engage in all of them.

1. **Planning**: This is the initial, and often, most crucial step in management. It involves setting clear, realistic goals, and outlining the steps to achieve them. As a small business owner, you must undertake both short-term and long-term planning. You need to know where your business is heading and map out the path to get there.

2. **Organizing**: Once you've developed plans, you need to organize your resources effectively to carry out these plans. This includes structuring your organization, sourcing required resources, delegating responsibilities, and setting up channels of

communication.

3. **Staffing**: Recruiting, training, developing, and retaining employees are all vital to a business's success. For small business owners, this involves not only hiring competent people but also fostering a positive work environment that encourages personal and professional growth.

4. **Leading**: As a leader, you influence your staff to achieve business objectives. Effective leaders motivate, communicate well, inspire trust, and, most importantly, lead by example.

5. **Controlling**: This vital function involves monitoring activities and making necessary adjustments to keep the business on track. As part of controlling, you will establish performance standards, measure actual performance, compare actual performance with these standards, and take corrective action whenever necessary.

3.2. Small Business: The Unique Challenges

Running a small business has its unique perks and challenges. As a small business owner, you can make decisions quickly without having to go through layers of approval. However, you're also the one solely responsible for the success or failure of your business.

On the positive side, your business can adapt to changes in the market environment faster than larger organizations. Still, it may struggle with issues regarding limited human and financial resources.

Understanding these challenges is essential to building managerial skills relevant to a small business atmosphere.

3.3. Entrepreneurship: The Spirit of Small Business

Entrepreneurship serves as the backbone of small business management. It's the driving force that motivates you to take calculated risks in the pursuit of new opportunities. Most small businesses are born out of an entrepreneurial spark - an innovative idea or a novel solution to a problem.

3.3.1. Traits of Successful Entrepreneurs

Successful entrepreneurs often share several distinct characteristics:

1. **Resilience**: Entrepreneurship is a journey littered with setbacks and failures. A successful entrepreneur is one who is resilient and sees failures as learning opportunities.

2. **Creativity**: Entrepreneurs are innovators. They view the world from a different angle and see opportunities where others don't.

3. **Vision**: Successful entrepreneurs have a clear vision for their business. They know what they want to achieve and how to get there.

4. **Flexibility**: The business landscape is constantly changing. Entrepreneurs need to be highly adaptable and ready to change course when necessary.

3.4. Legal Structures of Small Businesses

A foundational aspect of managing a small business is understanding the legal structures at your disposal. The structure you choose will impact your business operations in several ways, including taxation, required paperwork, and personal liability.

There are four primary types of legal structures:

1. **Sole Proprietorship**: This is the simplest structure, where the business is owned and managed by one individual. The owner assumes all risks and rewards of the business.

2. **Partnership**: A partnership involves two or more people who share the profits and losses of the business. All partners are legally liable for the actions of any one of the partners.

3. **Ltd. Company (LLC)**: This structure combines the features of corporations and partnerships. Owners enjoy limited personal liability and flexible income distribution.

4. **Corporation**: A corporation is a separate legal entity owned by shareholders. Luckily, the complex legal and financial requirements of corporations often make them unsuitable for small businesses.

3.5. Financing and Capital Management

Financing is a critical aspect to consider when managing a small business. Capital management involves the acquisition, allocation, and control of financial resources — and the ability to monitor, manage and control your outflows and inflows accurately.

There are numerous options for small business financing, including personal savings, business loans, angel investors, venture capitalists, and crowd funding platforms. It's crucial to find the appropriate financing mode that suits your business model, strategy, and long-term goals.

3.6. Early Stage and Rapid Growth

In the early stages, most small businesses consume more resources than they produce, hence the need for financing. During this phase, it's crucial to keep tight control over costs and focus on developing a profitable business model.

However, as your business grows, you must be able to manage rapid growth. Businesses that grow too fast might face issues with quality control, staffing, and finance management. As a small business manager, you need to balance the company's growth against its ability to successfully manage expanding operations.

The journey of small business management is undoubtedly rewarding, imbued with challenges to overcome and opportunities to grasp. Hopefully, this chapter has provided you with a clear understanding of the foundational principles underpinning small business management, and you're prepared to embark on your enterprise voyage.

Chapter 4. Business Planning and Strategy Development

Understanding the significance of a well-structured business plan and strategies to develop one is vital. A business plan is an in-depth exploration of your business purpose, targets, and methods for achieving your goals. It's more than a document; it's a map guiding your enterprise toward desired results, while coping with unforeseen hurdles along the way. Successful strategy development, on the other hand, is about connecting the dots between goals and actions, creating a robust path to success.

4.1. The Significance of Business Planning

Imagine setting out on a journey without a map, direction, or a destination. It's risky and nebulous, most likely leading you in circles. That's what operating a business without a plan is like. A clear and concise business plan serves as an indispensable tool for decision-making and fostering alignment among team members.

Business planning helps in risk mitigation, establishes a clear route to achieving your goals, provides a benchmark for measuring success, and is essential for securing investment. Most importantly, it allows you to understand your business from all perspectives.

4.2. Components of a Successful Business Plan

The quintessential business plan includes the following key sections:

1. Executive Summary: An overview of your business and plans. It

should be concise, engaging, and encompass your business's broad picture.

2. Company Description: Detailed insight into what your business does and the problem it solves.

3. Market Analysis: An in-depth examination of your industry, market, and competitors.

4. Organization and Management Structure: An outline of your business's organizational structure and the management team.

5. Product Line or Services: Detailed description of your products or services and their benefits.

6. Marketing and Sales Strategy: How you plan to market your business and your sales strategy.

7. Funding Request: If seeking funding, this section details your funding requirements.

8. Financial Projections: Detailed projections of your business's future financial health.

9. Appendix: An optional section that includes resumes and permits.

4.3. The Process of Building a Business Plan

Business plans are not born overnight. It's a meticulous process that requires introspection, market analysis, and financial projection. Here's the process for building a distinctive business plan.

1. Identify Your Business Purposes: Start by identifying exactly why you are preparing a business plan. Is it to guide your strategic direction, or is it aimed at investors? Your purpose will dictate the direction and depth of your plan.

2. Profile Your Company: Provide a snapshot of your business— who runs it, what services or products you offer, and who your

customers are.

3. Research the Market: Understand your operating environment. Evaluate competitors, market size, industry trends, and target demographics.

4. Identify Marketing and Sales Strategies: Identify the best marketing channels to reach your customers and outline your sales strategy.

5. Document Operational Processes: Detail how your business runs from day to day, highlight the roles and responsibilities of your team.

6. Develop Financial Projections: Anticipate revenues, expenses, and cash flow for the next 3–5 years.

7. Review and Refine: Continually read through, critique, and refine your plan. A business plan should be a living document, adapting with your business.

4.4. Strategy Development: More than Just Planning

With a business plan in place, your thoughts should shift toward strategy development. Where planning identifies 'what' you want to achieve, strategy dictates 'how' to get there. This entails determining your unique value proposition, identifying key performance indicators, carrying out a SWOT analysis, formulating strategic priorities, and developing an implementation plan.

The crucial elements of a strategic plan include vision, mission, strategic priorities, implementation plan, and performance measures. Unlike a business plan, a strategic plan is all-encompassing, guiding businesses not only in what they want to achieve but how they will do so.

4.5. The Process of Developing a Business Strategy

Creating a successful business strategy requires a systematic approach. Here's a step-by-step guide.

1. Set Vision and Mission: Your vision statement should outline what your business aspires to become in the future. A mission statement, on the other hand, should explain why your business exists and what it hopes to achieve in the short-term.

2. Identify Strategic Objectives: Set clear, realistic, and challenging objectives that align with your business mission.

3. Tactical Plans and Actions: Convert your objectives into actionable plans and assign responsibilities.

4. Performance Measures: Establish measures to assess your progress towards your objectives.

5. Execute and Evaluate: Implement your strategy, monitor progress, and make changes as necessary.

Whether beginning a start-up or planning to expand an established business, remember that success lies in thoughtful planning and strategic development. Equipped with the right strategies, an entrepreneur is on the pathway to a fruitful and sustainable business journey. Now you've understood the importance of a business plan and strategy development, let's move onto how you can use this knowledge to start building your wealth. Roll up your sleeves—it's time to make your money work for you!

Chapter 5. Mastering Cash Flow in Small Businesses

Managing cash flow effectively is one of the most critical tasks for a small business owner. It's not necessarily about making profits right away, but ensuring that the amount of cash coming into your business is greater than the amount of cash going out. This means keeping your income high and your expenses low. With a positive cash flow, you can meet your financial obligations, invest to grow your business, and ultimately, build wealth.

5.1. Understanding Cash Flow

At the most basic level, cash flow is the movement of money in and out of your business. Cash inflows generally come from activities such as sales of goods or services, sale of assets, borrowing from lenders, or investments from owners. On the other hand, cash outflows might arise from expenses such as inventory purchases, salaries and wages, rent, utilities, repayments of debts, and business investments.

Monitoring these cash inflows and outflows will provide a clear picture of your financial position and help you make informed decisions about your business operations. It's not enough to rely solely on your income statement and balance sheet. These financial statements may show a profitable business, but if your cash outflows exceed your cash inflows, your business is in a cash flow crunch.

5.2. Cash Flow Analysis

To effectively manage your cash flow, it's essential to conduct a regular cash flow analysis. This process involves tracking your cash inflows and outflows over a particular period, often on a monthly basis. You'll need to record all of your income and expenses, categorize them, and tabulate the total amounts.

Month	Cash Inflows	Cash Outflows	Net Cash Flow
January	$10,000	$8,000	$2,000
February	$15,000	$10,000	$5,000
March	$10,000	$12,000	-$2,000

Net Cash Flow = Cash Inflows - Cash Outflows

By maintaining this table you'll be able to identify patterns, examine seasonality, and predict future cash flows. Doing so enables you to be proactive about managing your finances, instead of reacting to financial problems after they've occurred.

5.3. Improving Cash Flows

Several strategies can improve the cash flow of your small business. Here are some of them:

1. Invoicing promptly and accurately: For service-based businesses, ensuring you get paid for your work in a timely manner is key. Make sure you send out invoices promptly after completing your work, and follow up on payments that aren't made on time.

2. Tightening credit terms: If you extend credit to your customers, consider tightening your credit terms. This might mean reducing the time frame for payment, requiring a deposit, or running credit checks on new clients.

3. Applying for funding: If needed, consider applying for small business loans or lines of credit. This can provide a much-needed cash injection when trying to grow your business.

4. Reducing expenses: Continually look for ways to reduce unnecessary expenses. This might mean renegotiating contracts

with vendors, optimizing utility usage, or streamlining your operations for more efficiency.

5. Boosting sales: Perhaps the most apparent way to increase your cash flow is by boosting your sales. Consider ways to attract more customers, such as marketing promotions, expanding your range of products or services, or entering new markets.

Remember, improving your cash flow is often about myriad little changes that add up to a big difference.

5.4. Cash Flow Forecasting

Cash flow forecasting is another key element in mastering cash flow management, allowing you to anticipate future scenarios, and plan accordingly.

Here's how you can craft a basic cash flow forecast:

Month	Estimated Cash Inflows	Estimated Cash Outflows	Estimated Net Cash Flow
Next Month	$12,000	$9,000	$3,000
Following Month	$15,000	$10,000	$5,000
After Two Months	$13,000	$11,000	$2,000

Estimated Net Cash Flow = Estimated Cash Inflows - Estimated Cash Outflows

A well-prepared forecast serves as a warning system, providing you with the opportunity to resolve any potential cash shortfalls in advance. It can help you identify when additional funding may be needed or when surplus cash will be available to reinvest back into the business.

5.5. Building a Cash Reserve

Building a cash reserve is a vital part of maintaining healthy cash flow. It ensures that you have a safety net to cover unexpected expenses or financial downturns. A healthy cash reserve is typically enough to cover three to six months' worth of business expenses. This reserve can provide you with financial security and allow for growth opportunities, letting your small business thrive, beating the odds, and building wealth over time.

Mastering cash flow management in your small business isn't a one-and-done task. It calls for regular monitoring, careful planning, and making adjustments as the business landscape changes. It's the key to growing your business sustainably and building lasting wealth. But remember, every small business is unique, and so are its financial circumstances. What works for one may not work for another. So, always tailor these strategies to fit your enterprise's distinctive needs.

Chapter 6. Modern Investment Models and Their Implications

Investing in the contemporary world is more than just picking stocks and hoping for the best. Modern investment models have revolutionized the way we approach investing by providing a mathematical and theoretical approach to estimating risk and expected return. These models have reshaped financial markets, investment strategies, and the overall global economy. While their complexities may seem daunting at first, understanding these models and their implications can unlock substantial wealth growth potential for individual and institutional investors alike.

6.1. The Efficient Market Hypothesis

The Efficient Market Hypothesis (EMH) is a bedrock of modern investment theory. Proposed by Eugene Fama in the 1960s, it postulates that all available information is immediately and accurately reflected in security prices. Consequently, this implies that it's nearly impossible to achieve consistent above-average returns without taking on above-average risk.

Despite criticism, EMH has significantly influenced investment strategies. It has led to the popularity of passive investing, where investors buy a representative benchmark, like an index fund, instead of trying to outperform the market. It also underscores the importance of diversification, as the inherent market risk, also known as systematic risk, cannot be eliminated, only managed.

6.2. The Capital Asset Pricing Model

One of the essential modern investment models is the Capital Asset Pricing Model (CAPM). The CAPM is used to determine a theoretically appropriate required rate of return on an asset. In this model, the expected return of an asset is a function of the risk-free rate, the asset's sensitivity to the overall market (beta), and the expected market return.

By using the CAPM, investors can calculate the expected return for an asset given its beta and make decisions about whether or not to add it to their portfolio. While this model has its limitations, it provides a technical foundation for modern portfolio theory and remains employed in financial decision-making, risk analysis, and valuation of securities.

6.3. Modern Portfolio Theory

Modern Portfolio Theory (MPT) promotes investment diversification to optimize returns for a given level of market risk. Harry Markowitz introduced this theory in 1952, winning a Nobel Prize for his work. According to MPT, it's not enough to look at the expected risk and return of one particular stock. By investing in more than one stock, an investor can reap the benefits of diversification — primary among them, a reduction in the riskiness of the portfolio.

MPT models portfolios as a weighted combination of assets. The goal is to find the set of weights that minimizes the volatility for a given expected return, forming the efficient frontier. Any point along this frontier represents a potentially optimal portfolio.

6.4. The Black-Scholes Model

The Black-Scholes Model, another cornerstone of modern finance, provides a theoretical estimate of the price of European-style options and derivatives. The model, developed by economists Fischer Black and Myron Scholes, with notable contributions from Robert Merton, is perhaps the world's best-known options pricing model.

Black-Scholes assumes that financial markets are efficient, and it considers factors such as the risk-free interest rate, the time to expiry of the option, the strike price, the price of the underlying asset, and the volatility of the underlying asset. This model has spurred the growth of options and derivatives trading, and while it may not be fully applicable in all market conditions, it remains standard in the field of financial derivatives.

6.5. Artificial Intelligence and Machine Learning

The recent advent of Artificial Intelligence (AI) and Machine Learning (ML) in finance is yet another leap forward in investment methodology. These technologies use substantial data sets and employ intricate algorithms to forecast market trends, identify investment opportunities, and manage risks.

ML can parse through substantial amounts of financial data to identify patterns not discernible by human analysts. Further, AI can learn from past financial data and successively improve its predictive capabilities, hence making it an increasingly essential tool in modern investing.

6.6. Implications of Modern Investment Models

Modern investment models have significantly impacted the financial world. They have led to the development of numerous financial services, from index funds to options, and have shaped regulatory practices. However, these models come with implications.

One such implication is that they assume market efficiency, which, in reality, is not always the case due to factors such as investor irrationality, constraints on short selling, and information asymmetry. Moreover, the increased digitization of finance and the use of AI and ML are creating new areas of risk, including data breaches and ethical issues.

The most successful investors understand these models and balance their benefits against their limitations. This knowledge allows informed decision-making, risk management, and ultimately, wealth creation.

Chapter 7. Unlocking the Power of the Stock Market

Financial security and freedom are derived from various sources, among which the stock market plays a pivotal role. Understanding how to strategically invest in stocks can ultimately lift your wealth-building strategy to the highest echelons.

Getting started in the stock market can indeed be daunting. However, with an effective framework, a solid understandings of the basics, and a good measure of discipline, this seemingly ominous task can become your pathway to making your money work more effectively for you.

7.1. The Basics of Stock Market Investing

When you purchase shares of a company's stock, you are essentially buying a piece of that business, thereby becoming a shareholder. Stocks represent ownership in the company and basic equity, which means you may be eligible to claim a part of the company's assets and earnings.

The stock market operates on the basic principles of supply and demand. A company's stock price can rise or fall based on its financial health and market economy. If a company is performing well and offering strong forecasts for future performance, demand for its shares will increase, which will push the stock price up.

As an investor, your goal should be to buy shares when prices are low and sell them when prices are high. However, a key strategy to get ahead in the stock market is to avoid timing the market. Rather, focus on your long-term financial goals and stay invested for the long haul.

7.2. Fundamental Analysis Vs. Technical Analysis

Two primary methods are used to estimate the true value of a company: Fundamental Analysis and Technical Analysis. Choosing which path you want to take is vital to your investment journey.

Fundamental analysis involves examining a company's finances — also known as financial ratio analysis. You'll analyze the income statement, balance sheet, and cash flow statement. Key ratios to consider are Current Ratio, Quick Ratio, Debt-Equity Ratio, Return on Equity (ROE), Price-Earnings (P/E) ratio, etc.

Technical analysis, on the other hand, involves evaluating the company's charts and historical data to identify patterns. It foregoes the exact numerical data and focuses on the statistical trends gathered from price and volume. Some popular patterns used in this synergy include the Head and Shoulders pattern, Candlestick patterns, MACD, RSI, etc.

7.3. The Art of Diversification

Investing in a single stock may lead to higher profits if the company performs exceptionally well. However, this strategy can be risky, as the downside potential is equally significant. Therefore, spreading your investments across multiple different types of investments, known as diversification, can balance out potential risks.

One way to do this is by investing in mutual funds or exchange-traded funds (ETFs). These encompass a blend of stocks from various companies, thereby spreading your risk over multiple investments. Other ways of diversification include investing in multiple sectors or industries and adhering to a global investing strategy.

7.4. Implementing Stop-Loss Orders

The concept of a stop-loss order is straightforward; this investment strategy protects you from potential losses. A stop-loss order automatically sells your stocks when they fall to a certain price. This strategy can prevent further losses in case of a severe market downturn.

Remember that stop-loss orders are not perfect and may have their disadvantages. Sometimes, the market can fluctuate drastically, resulting in your stocks being sold at a price considerably less than your stop-loss price.

7.5. Rebalancing Your Portfolio

After creating a diversified portfolio, another crucial step is to regularly review and make necessary adjustments. This process, known as rebalancing, inhibits your portfolio from becoming too exposed to one asset.

It's important to remember to rebalance only when necessary and to remain patient. Over-managing your investments can lead to unnecessary transaction costs and potential tax consequences.

Remember, investing in the stock market involves risks, and the value of investments can go down as well as up. As such, always ensure you have a well-balanced portfolio and consider obtaining financial advice, especially if you're new to investing.

Unlocking the power of the stock market is like acquiring a new language—the initial stages can be challenging, but with persistence and patience, the rewards can be immense. This chapter provided a foundation and offered you insight into navigating the world of stock market investing. Your journey has just begun. Continue learning, stay tenacious, and the sky can be your limit!

Chapter 8. Real Estate Investment: A Goldmine in Disguise

Real estate, often considered the cornerstone of a healthy investment portfolio, is known to provide consistent returns and excellent overall value. Over time, investing in real estate has proven to be a powerful strategy for wealth creation.

8.1. The Concept of Real Estate Investment

Investing in real estate is far more complex than simply purchasing a property and waiting for its value to increase. Understanding the marketplace, evaluating property values, assessing market trends, and negotiating deals are all crucial aspects of the real estate investment business.

Real estate investment involves the purchase, ownership, management, rental, or sale of property for profit. Instead of buying a property to use as a primary residence, these properties are bought to earn returns through rental income, appreciation, or both. A good investor is able to identify potential market opportunities and make strategic decisions, keeping long-term profitability in mind.

8.2. Why Real Estate Investment

Now, why should you consider real estate as a part of your investment plan? There are several reasons:

- Steady Cash Flow: Rental properties can generate a steady income. This can serve as a constant stream of cash flow that is higher than typical stock dividend yields.

- Appreciation: In the long run, real estate property values tend to increase, leading to capital gains for the owner.

- Diversification Potential: Real estate has a weak correlation with other major asset classes. This can enhance portfolio diversification and can potentially lower portfolio risk.

- Tax Benefits: There are numerous tax benefits associated with real estate investments, including depreciation and mortgage interest deductions.

- Use of Leverage: Real estate allows the use of leverage, which means investors can use various financing methods to buy a property, thereby increasing the potential return on investment.

8.3. Different Methods of Real Estate Investing

There are fundamentally four ways to invest in real estate:

1. Rental Properties: This is the most common method of real estate investing. Investors purchase a property and rent it out to tenants, earning monthly rental income.

2. Real Estate Investment Groups: These are like mutual funds for rental properties. If you want to own a rental, but don't want the hassle of being a landlord, this might be the right choice for you.

3. Real Estate Investment Trusts (REITs): A REIT is created when a corporation uses investors' money to purchase and operate income properties. This is perfect for investors looking for easy entry into real estate investment.

4. Real Estate Trading: This is the wild side of real estate investing. Also known as flipping, it involves buying a property, ideally improving it, and selling it for a profit within a short time.

8.4. Assessing a Real Estate Investment

Analyzing an investment opportunity in real estate is primordial. Successful real estate investing is all about buying at the right price and selling at the right time. Here are some key elements you should consider:

- Location: This is perhaps the most crucial factor. The ideal property is located in a growing community with good schools, amenities, and transportation.

- Market Trends: Understand the current market trends, including any changes in customer behavior or the economy, and how they are likely to affect the property.

- Cash Flow & Growth Potential: Look at the potential rental income, operating expenses, and property value growth rate.

- Property Condition: Factor in repair and improvement costs when determining the property's value.

To conclude, real estate can indeed be a goldmine if handled with care and strategic planning. However, it is important to carry out your own thorough research and possibly consult with a real estate investment advisor before diving into the field. It's not a guaranteed path to easy riches, but with knowledge, expertise, and some resilience, it's a highly profitable investment avenue.

Now is the time to seize the opportunity and start building your real estate portfolio. With the right strategy and a little patience, you can truly turn real estate into a goldmine!

Chapter 9. Estate Planning and Wealth Preservation

Estate planning is a crucial but often overlooked component of wealth management and preservation. This aspect involves transferring an individual's wealth and assets in a way that aligns with their wishes. Effective estate planning is not only about ensuring that your heirs receive maximum assets with minimal tax liability, but it's also about making sure these assets are managed prudently in your absence.

9.1. Understanding Estate Planning

Estate planning involves the development and implementation of legal, financial, and logistical plans to manage an individual's assets upon his or her incapacitation or death. These assets can include bank accounts, real estate, stocks, life insurance policies, pensions, personal belongings, and even debts.

The purpose of estate planning is twofold: it ensures that your beneficiaries are well-cared for in accordance with your wishes, and it strategically structures your estate to minimize the tax burden upon transfer.

9.2. The Importance of Last Will and Testament

A Last Will and Testament is a legal document where you can designate who you want to inherit your property, name a guardian for your minor children and nominate an executor to wind down your affairs. If a person passes away without a will, their assets are distributed according to state law, which may not always coincide with the individual's intended wishes.

9.3. Utilizing Trusts in Estate Planning

Trusts are another vital instrument for estate planning. A trust is a legal relationship where a person or institution (the trustee) holds and manages assets for the benefit of another person or persons (the beneficiaries). Trusts can help avoid probate, provide for loved ones who are minors, disabled, or inexperienced with financial matters, and can offer significant tax advantages.

9.4. Planning for Incapacity

Incapacity planning is a critical component of any comprehensive estate plan. It encompasses documents like durable powers of attorney and advance health care directives that allow you to designate individual(s) who can make financial and medical decisions on your behalf if ever you become unable to do so yourself.

9.5. Tax Implications and Estate Planning

Upon death, a person's estate may be subject to estate tax, and the individual inheriting the property could potentially be liable for inheritance tax. The former is a tax on the right to transfer property at your death, while the latter is a state tax that some heirs must pay on the assets they inherit. Effective estate planning can help minimize these tax burdens.

9.6. Assets Not Subject to Estate Plan

Certain assets, such as life insurance payouts and retirement plans, are not governed by your will or trust. Those are generally transferred by beneficiary designation, meaning whoever is listed on the policy or plan will receive the asset directly, bypassing your estate.

9.7. Implementing Buy-Sell Agreements for Business Owners

If you own a business, your estate plan should incorporate a buy-sell agreement. A buy-sell agreement specifies how a partner's share of a business may be reassigned if that partner dies or otherwise leaves the business. It is a legally binding agreement between co-owners of a business that governs the situation if a co-owner dies or is otherwise forced to leave the business, or chooses to leave the business.

9.8. Regular Reviews and Updates of Your Estate Plan

As years pass and life events occur (birth, death, marriage, divorce, business startups, etc.), you'll need to periodically review and update your estate plan to ensure it aligns with your personal, financial, and familial evolution.

In conclusion, estate planning is an integral part of wealth management and preservation. With careful and considerate planning, you can ensure your loved ones are taken care of in your absence and that your wealth and assets are distributed according to your wishes. Remember, it's never too early to start strategizing and planning for the future. It's not just about dividing up belongings; it's about peace of mind, legacy preservation, and easing the administrative burden for those you leave behind.

Chapter 10. Crypto-assets: Navigating the New Frontiers of Investment

Cryptocurrency is revolutionizing the world of finance. As an emerging asset class, it offers unique investment opportunities that diverge from traditional financial systems. Despite being relatively new, the crypto market's exponential growth has attracted a wide range of investors, all seeking to leverage the potential gains it represents.

10.1. Understanding Cryptocurrencies

To effectively invest in cryptocurrencies, an initial understanding of what they represent is fundamental. Cryptocurrencies are digital or virtual currencies that use cryptography for security. Unlike traditional money issued by central banks, these are decentralized and often issued by the development teams behind them.

The pioneer and most renowned of all cryptocurrencies is Bitcoin, developed in 2009 by an unknown person or group of people using the name Satoshi Nakamoto. The primary purpose of Bitcoin was to create a peer-to-peer electronic cash system, enabling online payments to be sent directly from one party to another without going through a financial institution.

Since Bitcoin's inception, thousands of other cryptocurrencies, often referred to as altcoins (alternative coins), have been developed, boasting different attributes and focusing on different use cases. Ethereum, for instance, introduced the concept of "smart contracts," facilitating the automated execution of contracts when certain conditions are met.

10.2. Blockchain: The Underpinning Technology

Cryptocurrencies are built on a technology known as blockchain. A blockchain is essentially a digital ledger of transactions that are duplicated and distributed across an entire network of computer systems (nodes). Each block in a chain contains multiple transactions, and every time a new transaction is added to a blockchain, a record of that transaction is updated on each participant's ledger.

Blockchain's decentralization and immutability make it incredibly secure, providing a high level of trust and transparency in recording transactions. This disruptive technology is not merely limited to finance, but is finding extensive usage across various industries such as healthcare, supply chain, and real estate.

10.3. Investing in Cryptocurrencies

Cryptocurrency investing is quite different from traditional investing, and can be a high-risk, high-return affair. To venture into this space, an investor must understand the nature of cryptocurrencies, their volatility, liquidity concerns, and, importantly, regulatory complexities.

The dramatic rises and precipitous drops in the value of various cryptocurrencies have highlighted their volatility. This volatility can present substantial potential gain, but it also carries significant risk, and investors must be prepared for the possibility of losing their entire investment.

Liquidity can also be an issue with certain cryptocurrencies. While significant cryptocurrencies like Bitcoin and Ethereum are easily tradeable, smaller, lesser-known cryptocurrencies may not be as liquid.

The regulatory environment surrounding cryptocurrency is also rapidly evolving. As laws and regulations vary widely by jurisdiction, it is crucial that prospective investors understand the regulatory landscape and implications of their investments.

10.4. Diversifying Portfolio with Crypto-assets

Including cryptocurrency in your portfolio provides a hedge against traditional investment classes. It's akin to the diversification of investing in gold as an asset class that doesn't correlate directly with stock markets. Yet, it's also essential to understand that high returns come with high risks.

Crypto-assets should be a portion of your investment portfolio that matches your risk appetite. The conventional wisdom for diversified investing – not to put all your eggs in one basket – holds true in the context of cryptocurrencies. Diversifying among a blend of asset classes can likely weather the storm of short-term fluctuations in individual investments.

10.5. Bitcoin & Beyond: Evaluating Crypto-assets

Vetting potential crypto-assets for investment purposes should be a process as rigorous as that applied to more traditional investments. It's important to conduct a fundamental analysis of each cryptocurrency you plan on adding to your portfolio. This analysis should focus on total circulating supply, market capitalization, the credibility of the team behind the coin, the problem they're trying to solve, and the coin's real-world applications.

Bitcoin, due to its pioneer status and broad acceptance, is often considered a safe investment compared to other cryptocurrencies. Altcoins, though riskier, present opportunities for higher returns. These include platforms like Ethereum, utility tokens like Binance Coin, and tokens that represent an entirely new category such as Chainlink, a decentralized oracle network.

10.6. Navigating Crypto Exchanges

The primary way to acquire cryptocurrencies is through crypto exchanges - platforms where you can buy, sell, and hold cryptocurrencies. Notable crypto exchanges include Coinbase, Bittrex, and Binance. It's important for investors to understand how these platforms work, the fees involved in transactions, and the security measures they have in place to protect the assets of their users.

In conclusion, though investing in cryptocurrencies entails its unique set of risks, the potential for substantial returns makes it an asset class that's worth considering. However, the key to successful investment is understanding the landscape, carrying out comprehensive research, assessing potential risks, and making decisions that align with individual financial goals and risk tolerance. Navigating the new frontier of investment that cryptocurrencies represent can be daunting, but with the right knowledge and strategies, it can lead you on a path toward financial independence. Always remember, the world of cryptocurrency is not a race, but a journey. Pace yourself.

Chapter 11. Building a Diverse and Resilient Investment Portfolio

Understanding the importance of setting up a diverse and resilient portfolio cannot be overstated. Diversification is essentially about 'not putting all your eggs in one basket.' But, how exactly do you start diversifying your investments and building a resilient portfolio? This chapter gives an in-depth exploration into the strategies and methods.

11.1. The Concept of Diversification

Diversification is the practice of spreading your investments around so that your exposure to any one type of asset is limited. This tactic aims to maximize return by investing in different areas that would each respond differently to the same event. Most investment professionals agree that diversification is the most important component of reaching long-range financial goals while minimizing risk.

11.2. How Diversification Works

In diversifying your portfolio, the goal is creating a balance that can withstand shifts in the economy, reducing the risk that your entire portfolio will lose value if one sector underperforms. Essentially, if some of your investments are doing poorly, you'll be in a position to counterbalance the effect through others that are performing well.

As an analogy, consider a well-balanced meal with variations in food items. If your meal comprises only carbohydrates and lacks proteins, vitamins, or fats, the deficiency of these vital nutrients can make your body system vulnerable to ailments. Similarly, if your portfolio comprises only one investment type (like stocks), it becomes weak and exposed to the volatility and unpredictability in the financial market.

11.3. Importance of a Diverse Portfolio

A well-diversified portfolio is more stable due to the decreased risk of potential loss. By spreading investments across various financial instruments, economic sectors, or other categories, investors protect themselves from disastrous outcomes within a single sector. This approach asserts the notion that not all types of investments gain or lose at the same time or at the same pace, reducing the potential for a large loss within your portfolio.

11.4. Building a Diverse Portfolio

Understanding how and where to diversify can be daunting. Here are some key ways to diversify your portfolio.

Asset allocation: The practice of dividing investments among different asset categories, such as stocks, bonds, and cash. Each asset class has different levels of return and risk, so each will behave differently over time.

Geographical diversification: Consider asset allocation but on a global scale. Economic downturns can hit nations differently, so spreading investments around can offset the risks faced with an individual country's market.

Sector diversification: Different sectors or industries within an economy have unique factors that affect their performance. Diversify your stocks across several sectors such as technology, utilities, healthcare, and financials, among others.

11.5. The Concept of Resilience in Investments

Resilience in an investment refers to its ability to recover from or adjust easily to misfortune or change, thus limiting potential losses. Resilient investments are those that offer stable returns despite market volatility. Fixed income bonds, value stocks, and index funds are often considered resilient investments due to their slow but steady growth patterns.

11.6. Building a Resilient Portfolio

Building a resilient investment portfolio involves assessing the market, choosing the mix of assets, and diligent oversight to ensure your investments are performing as expected. Here are steps to creating a resilient portfolio:

Analyze the market trends: Knowledge is power when it comes to investment. Understanding market trends and economic indicators can help you anticipate potential issues and leverage opportunities.

Asset allocation: The right mix of assets can help you build a portfolio that can stand the test of time.

Maintaining liquidity: Ensure you have enough readily accessible funds to cover any unexpected expenses or losses without having to sell your investments at a potential loss.

Diligent oversight: Regularly review your portfolio to ensure it is performing as expected and adjust as necessary.

In conclusion, a strong, diverse, and resilient investment portfolio offers stability and potential growth during economic uncertainty. Balancing your investment risks with diversification and resilience can help you reach your financial goals safely and effectively.

www.ingramcontent.com/pod-product-compliance
Lightning Source LLC
Chambersburg PA
CBHW072218290526
45794CB00007B/2796